SHE'S POSSIBLE

Find Your Irresistible You

Dr. Trillion Small

They Speak Publishing

REVIEW

WHAT DO YOU THINK OF THE BOOK SO FAR?

Thanks so much for purchasing this book! We'd love to hear about your experience thus far.

We invite you to write a review on Amazon.

To show our appreciation we will email you a free copy of the colorful Digital PDF version of "While Quarantined". An e-workbook for those looking to grow emotionally, mentally, and Spiritually.

You can get a sneak peek of the inside of the digital E-workbook at trillionsmall.com/singlewhilequarantined

WRITE A REVIEW STEPS

1. Write a review on Amazon. To write a review on Amazon simply locate your order and click "Write a Product Review"
2. If you did not purchase the book from Amazon you can still leave a review by simply finding the book on Amazon and scrolling to the very bottom of the product page and clicking "Write a Customer Review"
3. Once you write the review. Visit trillionsmall.com/reviews or scan the QR code below with the camera on your phone.
4. Fill out the online form.
5. All done! We will double-check that your review was posted to Amazon and we will then send you your gift via email.

Thank you again. May this book add value to your life.

Scripture Foundation for *She's Possible*

*"Do not let your adornment be merely outward—
arranging the hair, wearing gold, or putting on fine
apparel* [4] *rather let it be the hidden person of the
heart, with the incorruptible beauty of a gentle and
quiet spirit, which is very precious in the sight of
God."*

– I Peter 3:3-4

She's Possible

Find Your Irresistible You

© 2018, 2019 by Trillion Small

Published by They Speak Publishing, Dallas, Texas

The names, details, and circumstances may have been changed to protect the privacy of those mentioned in this publication.

Headshots by Kauwuane Burton

Printed in the United States of America

ISBB:9781977021069

Other Books By Trillion Small

Owning Possible: Your Guide to Making the Impossible Possible!

The Caged Free Heart: Letting Go of the Past that Incarcerates (2nd Edition)

Internal Navigator: Basic Steps to Get You from Point A to Point B in Your Life (2nd Edition)

Dedication

I dedicate this book to my big sister, Felicia. God has gifted you with so many amazing gifts. You are super creative with your hands and you definitely have what it takes to be a *She's Possible* woman.

Table of Contents

INTRODUCTION

★★★

I wrote the book *She's Possible* to empower women. I have encountered so many amazing women in my life thus far. Some are doing mind-blowing things while others are trying to figure out how to tap into her potential. I wrote this book for both categories of women. It is my firm belief that no matter where you are in your life, if you can grasp a hold of these few principles, you will be unstoppable, irresistible, and a woman who is able to take what seems impossible and make it possible.

It is my hope that you will have found your irresistible self by the end of this book. I love this definition of "irresistible": *too powerful or convincing to be resisted*[1]. That's what I want for you!

I once heard a man say, "When you are attractive to God you are irresistible to man." This isn't just about being physically attractive and irresistible. You'll have to find another book to teach you how to do that. But this book is basically teaching you how to become so attractive to God that man [or woman] couldn't resist you if they tried. They will want you to have a seat at the table, they will want you to work with their company, they will want to be your friend, and they will want to simply be in your presence.

The scripture foundation for this book hits the nail on the head with this idea. Again, I Peter 3:3-4 says, *"Do not let your adornment be merely outward—arranging the hair, wearing gold, or putting on fine apparel* [4] *rather let it be the hidden person of the heart, with the incorruptible beauty of a gentle and quiet spirit, which is very precious in the sight of God."* This does not mean don't focus on looking presentable externally because you surely should care about that. But your external beauty is not what makes you attractive to God. I'm pretty sure it isn't the length of your extensions or your eyelashes that catches God's attention. Well unless He is looking saying, "What in the world, I did not create her with all of that extra stuff." Just kidding, I like fake eyelashes too. I like when they blow in the wind. Lol, ☺. Ok back to being serious.

God is attracted to your heart and ultimately that is our goal here. To become precious and pleasing in God's sight, and as a result, our heart will naturally draw favor, blessings, and increase in every area of our lives. So if you are ready, come and enter into my internal beauty salon and be prepared to get a total make over.

CHAPTER ONE

Find You

★★★

Who am I?

I have now watched the Disney movie Moana at least 327 times. I have zero kids, but I truly desire to be a screenplay writer for Disney one day, so I watch their movies to learn how they tell stories. That's my justification at least, and I'm sticking with it. But no seriously, I just love that movie! Spoiler alert. If you haven't seen it and didn't want to know the end, then go watch it and finish reading. In a nutshell Moana, the lead character goes on this long journey to restore the heart of Te Fiti, the mother island that brought life to all of the surrounding islands. The beauty of the islands, the greenery, the fish, and the produce was all because of her. But, someone stole her heart, and everything went downhill from that point. The islands were slowly dying because of it and it was Moana's sole mission to journey across the sea and restore her heart. This would then restore life back to the islands.

Moana's greatest external battle was with Teka, the lava monster. I'd call her Te Fiti's alter personality. Teka was a furious monster that destroyed anything that tried to come near Te Fiti. Come to find out, Teka WAS Te Fiti. Teka is who came out when someone stole Te Fiti's heart. Teka even wanted to destroy Moana even though she was only trying to help.

Fast forward. Moana now comes face to face with the monster and sang, "This is not who you are. You know who you are"[1]. Teka immediately ceased her pursuit and calmed herself down. She allowed Moana to restore her heart and once she had her heart back the hard lava shell that covered her entire body fell off, and Te Fiti, her true and authentic self, was revealed. Te Fiti took her rightful place back where she belonged and immediately began to bring life back to herself first and then to the surrounding islands. Moana's song quickly helped Teka to realize who she truly was. All she needed was that simple reminder of what was deep down on the inside of her. But knowing who we are isn't always that easy.

I believe one question that many of my clients have a difficult time answering when they first come to see me is "who are you?" They start off with their jobs or their roles, and I listen. But then I ask again, "but who are you? Apart from all of that, who are you at your core?" I then repeat a two-word phrase to them ten times and I ask them to just simply fill in the blank with whatever automatically comes to mind without thinking too hard. So I want you to try it too right now so grab a pen. Simply fill in the blank with whatever comes to mind. If "I don't know" comes up a few times then write that down in the blank as well and then move on to the next one. The goal is just to keep moving down the list until you get to 10.

So here we go.

1. I am _____.
2. I am _____.
3. I am _____.
4. I am _____.
5. I am _____.
6. I am _____.
7. I am _____.
8. I am _____.
9. I am _____.
10. I am _____.

There is no right or wrong answer obviously but here is an example of what I might see with a client.

1. I am… a mom.
2. I am… tired.
3. I am… angry.
4. I am… sad.
5. I am… I don't know.
6. I am… hurt.
7. I am… I don't know.
8. I am… hardworking.
9. I am… happy.
10. I am… strong.

About halfway, some find themselves getting emotional. I ask why and a common response is, "I just never realized that I truly do not know who I am." I then re-read the list back to them, and I ask them how true do they believe the positive ones to be. They often say that they don't believe them fully, but that is who they hope to become. This conversation usually happens in the first few sessions, so I then ask them, " are you willing to go on a journey to discover who you are?" And of course, they nod and say yes.

So I will ask you the same thing. Are you willing to go on this journey with me to discover who you are? If you read any further, I will take that as a yes. Don't be surprised though, if you start off feeling like you already know everything there is to know about yourself, only to discover that you have so much more to learn. That was the case for me at least and I am pretty self-aware, but I was in for an eye-opening journey when I finally decided to venture to find me. I believe that you will be too.

The Meaning Behind a Name

One of the very first questions we ask a person that we just meet is, "What is your name?" Names help you to identify with whom you are talking. And beyond that, I think that names should tell us more about the character of a person, about the direction that the person's life will go, or about the overall mantle or blessing which was assigned to their life. For example, they didn't just randomly name their child any ole thing in the Bible. Names had power and significance, and if it wasn't as "powerful", it at least told a story. Some told a good story while others told a not so good story.

For example, Leah's first three baby boy's names all tell the story of her longing to connect with her husband and her fourth tells the story of how she planned to focus on the Lord and give Him all the praise regardless of how her husband was treating her[2]. When you think about it, it doesn't seem like she was thinking about her kid's destiny, though, when she named them. She was thinking about herself and what she wanted with her husband. Have you ever felt like the "middle-man"; like the ping-pong that is hit back and forth between your parents but the focus is never really on you? I have had many clients tell me stories of how their mom would talk to them about their father and their father would talk to them about their mother and how each would send messages to each other through them. This is a tough role to play, and it is one that you should not have to play. You are not your parent's mediators, and you do have a role and function in life outside of being your parent's translators of information. You were not born just so that you could be there telephones. And if you are a mother, ask yourself, "Am I using my child just so that I can get close to, translate information to, or get back at (for whatever reason) their father?" Be honest. If so, please consider stopping for the sake of the child.

What about Jacob? He had to go through a whole name change[3]. God changed his name from Jacob, which meant supplantor and often called a "trickster" or "deceiver," to Israel, which meant he wrestled or struggled with God. The name change was wonderful but what I think is even more powerful is that he immediately took the revelation of the importance of names and renamed his twelfth son who was birthed right after this name change encounter. Jacob played no role in naming his other children, but he made sure that he did with this child. Let's look at it in Genesis 35:16-18, *"Then they journeyed from Bethel. And when there was but a little distance to go to Ephrath, Rachel labored in childbirth, and she had hard labor. [17] Now it came to pass, when she was in hard labor, that the midwife said to her, "Do not fear; you will have this son also." [18] And so it was, as her soul was departing (for she died), that she called his name Ben-Oni; but his father called him Benjamin."* His wife named the child Ben-Oni which means son of my sorrow but Jacob stepped in and said no his name is Benjamin, which means sons of the right hand.

Wow, just listen at the difference in those two names. They are completely different. One focuses on sorrow while the other focuses on strength. That is what Daddy God wants to do with you my sister friend! He wants to rename you! No longer will you be labeled by what you did or what happened to you! NO! You will now be called by what He calls you, and that is Love, The Apple of His Eye, Virtuous Woman, Daughter, and so many other beautiful names!

I just loved seeing the transition of names for the woman with the issue of blood too[4]. Up until her meeting with Jesus, she was defined by her issues. She was Ms. The Woman with the Issue of Blood, BUT when she encountered the great I AM He then changed it and called her Daughter. No longer did she have to be defined by her past but she could walk in boldness in her new identity and so can you!

What is Your Name?

So what about you? What have you been calling yourself lately? What are those subtle things that always pop in your head about yourself? And what do you subconsciously call yourself? I want you to think about this long and hard because whatever follows your "I am" statement is what you allow to define you.

What do you put after your "I am" statement? Think with me for a moment. When you first introduce yourself, you say, "Hi, I am_____" and you give them your name so that they can identify you. But what about those times that you've said I am stupid, I am not good enough, I am too fat/too skinny, I am too ugly, I am a burden, I am not loved, I am a liar, I am rejected, I am not wanted, I am broke, I am a poor writer/speaker/etc., I am _____. All of these names count too, and they truly do hurt you whether you know it or not.

Someone once asked me, "well what if you are those things?" and I could see their point, but I explained to them that there is a difference from telling a lie and being a liar. There is a difference between someone not loving you and you being an unlovable person. This may be dividing hairs now, but I truly do believe that what you put after your "I am" statements is what defines you. It all boils down to who you truly are at your CORE! Now if you are just a flat out liar, cheater, etc who does it all the time then ask the Lord to change your core. If He could do it for Jacob and Paul, the Christian killer, then He sure can do it for you too.

Don't Be What They Call You. Be YOU!

I use to call myself *I am* not good enough, *I am* not loved, and *I am* not wanted. But all of these names were lies! *I am* good enough, *I am* loved, *and I am* wanted. And after God gave me a lesson on names I immediately decided to "change my name"! No longer would I allow my circumstance or what people did to me define me. I took responsibility in changing my name, and you have the same responsibility. So please, watch your mouth. Watch what you say about yourself because you are listening!

Now let's take another lesson on this from the Disney movie Zootopia. One of the characters is a sly fox named Nick Wilde. All throughout the movie, he was slick and deceitful. In one of his vulnerable moments, he explains that he is the way he is because all his life people only viewed him to be sly and shifty, so he decided not to prove them wrong and just be what they perceived him to be. Thank goodness he met a new friend, who happened to be an underestimated bunny. She saw the good in him, and she helped him to "change his name" by helping him to change his identity. She basically showed him that he didn't have to be what people said about it. She showed him that he had a choice. And that choice starts with our words.

Watch Your Mouth

What we call ourselves (and others) has major impact, and it shapes our world; for the good or bad. For example, I've talked with some guys who were honest enough to say that he had cheated on his woman. I found some of their stories interesting because some of them said that they were always faithful until she kept blaming him for cheating when he wasn't. It seems like there is a case of Nick Wilde going on here.

No, I am not justifying his behavior and no I am not saying it is the woman's fault, but sometimes we can speak things over and over again until we reap the very words that we sowed and end up with a self-fulfilling prophecy. Women, we can be notorious for this. Thus we must do a better job at watching our mouths. Not just for ourselves and not just for our significant others but also for our children, our friends, and our community at large. Instead of calling your kids 'bad' call them 'well-behaved children of God'. Instead of calling your husband 'a no good for nothing man if he can call himself that', try calling him 'a faithful man after God's own heart!' Some would say, "well I just call it like I see it," And my response would then be, "that may be your problem." What if the way that you see it is all wrong? What if your negative doom and gloom view-point is killing the very people you love?!

I can't say this enough. Your words have power. So when you get ready to speak anything, ask yourself this, "is what is about to come out of my mouth what I truly want to see manifested?" If the answer is no then zip your mouth shut. When God opened His mouth, stuff happened. All He had to say was "let there be..." and whatever He said had to happen. None of it existed, but because He said it, His words then had to become a reality.

If you don't want to be sick, then don't say, "omg you make me sick!" If you aren't trying to rush your time here on earth, then don't say, "I'm dead." If you want your children to excel in all areas of life, then don't call them stupid. If you want to be a healthy weight, then stop looking in the mirror saying, "Wow, I'm so fat." I can go on and on, but you get the point. I know some of these are "slang" but don't even play around with slang! Your words are like a sword, so treat them accordingly! You don't just go around slinging a real sword all over the place aimlessly do you? No. Well, don't do your words that way either. Remember, your words help to shape your world.

You are Chosen

I can truly say that my life began to drastically change when I started to pay attention to what I was calling myself and replaced those negative "I am" statements with truth and life. It all started with a dream; as do most of my ah-ha revelation moments. A couple of years ago I had a very simple dream. In my dream, I picked up a folded piece of paper and on it read, Trillion means chosen, destined. End scene.

I can't recall what all was happening in my life at that time, but I know that it was a season where God was trying to teach me how to *be*. I was so focused on doing stuff that I was getting lost in the shuffle. I even minimized my name, Trillion, to mean something I wish to accomplish, which is a trillion dollars ☺. Don't get me wrong, that is still the end goal, but this dream truly opened my eyes to the importance of the meaning of names. Now of course if you were to Google the meaning of Trillion, I can guarantee you that the words chosen and destined are not words that will pop up unless it is my blog that I wrote in reference to my name.

Destined and chosen are names that reflect my core, regardless of what I do on the outside. And the same is true for you too. I Peter 2:9 reminds us, *"you are a chosen generation, a royal priesthood, a holy nation, His own special people, that you may proclaim the praises of Him who called you out of darkness into His marvelous light."* And Romans 8:29-30 reminds us, *"For whom He foreknew, He also predestined to be conformed to the image of His Son, that He might be the firstborn among many brethren. [30] Moreover whom He predestined, these*

He also called; whom He called, these He also justified; and whom He justified, these He also glorified."

The movie, Moana, did a phenomenal job depicting these two scriptures and showing what it is like to be called, chosen, and destined. Moana was about 12-18 months old when she had an encounter with the ocean. In this first encounter, the ocean chose her to be the one who would restore the heart back to Te Fiti. Now this is no surprise when you realize that her name Moana actually means ocean. Before she could even walk, she was called to the ocean. She was the chosen one. And like any good movie, the movie is pointless without a challenge to overcome. Her family tried to hinder her from becoming who she was called to be. Her father forbid her from going deep into the ocean and her mother even told her that who she desired to be just was not meant to be. Ouch. Thanks supportive parents. If it wasn't for her grandmother I don't think Moana would have realized she was the chosen one and that she had to fulfill her calling because everyone's life depended on it. Literally.

What it really boiled down to was Moana having to overcome not only her own fears but her parent's fears as well. I once heard someone say that the greatest challenge is not only overcoming your own comfort zone but also overcoming the comfort zone of those around you. At the end of the day we are fully responsible for taking ownership of our life and the direction that we will allow it to go. Of course with the realization that God guides our every step, but He guides our steps He doesn't make our steps for us so you still have a role to play here. Pick up your feet and put one foot in front of the other. That's your job.

We cannot use the excuse of, "they didn't believe in me or they told me I wasn't qualified!" Yes, I know there is power in support so if you don't have any cheerleaders in your corner then I will sign up to be one! YOU CAN DO IT YES

YOU CAN YOU CAN DO IT YES YOU CAN! And not only can you…but you must. We need what you have to offer. And YES what you have to offer is of GREAT significance so please do not minimize it.

Never Minimize Yourself

Speaking of minimization. Ladies, oh how I long for the day that we stop minimizing and overly critiquing who we are physically. I'm sure we all have done it. I'm not tall enough. I'm not thin enough. My hair isn't long enough. My natural hair coils are too tight. My eyelashes are too short. My skin complexion is too dark/light. My butt is too small. My boobs aren't big enough. My legs aren't pretty enough. My waist isn't small enough. My eyebrows aren't thick enough. My lips are too big/too small. And on and on and on and on. Now, there is nothing wrong with wanting to enhance what you already have but why do we feel the need to often bully ourselves? We would get mad and upset if someone else critiqued us the way we critique ourselves so why do we do it? I know I use to be my worst critic and I hated that I was but I never knew how to stop.

I recall being out at dinner a few years ago and the waitress looks at me and says, "you have pretty eyes." And my response literally was, "they are just brown." What in the world had gotten into my mind to tell me that brown was not pretty?! I figured if they weren't green, grey, or blue that they were just "basic." I left that restaurant actually disappointed in myself for minimizing my beauty! I made a commitment to myself that night to never minimize and critique who I am in such a negative and demeaning way again! I too hope that you will be able to look in the mirror and say I LOVE ALL OF ME BECAUSE GOD LOVES ALL OF ME!

Never Underestimate Your Abilities

I want to wrap this chapter up by encouraging you to take the time to reflect over just how much value and worth you have. I mean you are so stunning that after God created you He stepped back and said, Woah Man (wo-man)! Haha. Though that may have been super cheesy it is fundamentally true. When your heart, mind, and spirit fully align with God you become one of the most fierce and unstoppable women out there. I mean someone needs to bring you a cape already!

When you think about it, minimizing ourselves does not bring God the full glory. We bring Him the full glory when we allow Him to use us in the capacity that He so desires. And truthfully, to call bad what He has already called good is sort of like a slap in the face to the Creator and it is as if you are calling Him a lie.

When Moana's grandmother first told her
that she was chosen she questioned her calling just
like many of us have done. She wondered why the
ocean would choose a young girl who didn't even
know how to sail. She could have easily just said,
"you have the wrong girl" but she didn't. Well she
actually did towards the end but she was just so
physically and emotionally exhausted after losing
her first battle with Teka. But grandmamma comes
again and saves the day as she gently reminds her
who she is and what she has been chosen to do.
That gave her enough internal power to go and try
again to fulfill her destiny. Thank goodness for
grandmamma!

Who do you have in your inner circle to give
you a little pep talk in the event that you begin to
second guess your calling and begin to
underestimate yourself? We all need at least one
person who can remind us who we are and what we
were called to do! My mom is that person for me!
One day I called her feeling soooo disappointed in

myself after an interview. In my mind, I blew it! I called her telling her just how horrible I did and she quickly stopped me in my tracks and said, "woah wait a minute this is not my daughter talking!" She wouldn't let me underestimate my effectiveness no matter how much I wanted to gripe and complain about all the stuff I perceived I did wrong! She helped me to see the positives, helped me to quickly learn from what I perceived I did wrong, and she reminded me that I am cut out for this!

I, as your newest cheerleader say to you…YOU do have what it takes, YOU are cut out for this, YOU are good enough, YOU are chosen, YOU do have value, and YOU are worthy! Believe it deep in your spirit because it is true! Period. No ifs, ands, or buts.

Be Confident

I will say this and drop the mic for real this time. You are not competing with men. You are not even competing with other women. You are competing with inner YOU. If you truly believe that you are unstoppable and if you truly believe that you can do the impossible then no man or woman can hold you back. Only you can!

May I have a moment of confession? I use to never like being around other beautiful women. I use to be so insecure in myself that when I saw another woman walk in confidence I low key envied her. Her confidence brought out my insecurities. It wasn't until I truly became confident in who I was, that I began to truly be comfortable around other beautiful and confident women. I also stopped thinking that men were "holding us back."

Once I learned my secret sauce I knew that I didn't have to compete with a man's strength because I had my own! So I didn't want to "be like the boys." I have what they don't and if you are a woman, you also have what they don't and that thing is the secret sauce that makes you unstoppable and irresistible. What's the secret sauce you ask?

Shh. Don't tell anyone, but it is your captivating and wooing gentleness. Yep, that's the secret sauce! Turn on over to chapter two and let's talk about this secret sauce!

Reflection Time

An irresistible woman is one who is confident. She knows who she is and she doesn't allow anyone to tell her any different. An irresistible woman knows that she is called and she carries herself as such. She walks with her head held high because she realizes if she were to hang her head low, her queenly crown would fall off.

1. Do you know who are you are? Who are you at your core?

2. Do you know what you are designed for? Why were you chosen? Chosen to do what?

3. Sometimes we can be our own worst critics. In what ways have you minimized or underestimated your abilities? If you still do those things today, what are some steps that you can take to uplift yourself more instead of tearing yourself down? Who will hold you accountable?

CHAPTER TWO

Find Your Strength

Gentleness is Your Strength

I went to a relationship conference not too long ago and I found the Q&A session most interesting. Mainly because the types of questions asked, help me to discover the needs of the people. I then take that need and try to find a solution for it. One single lady raises her hand and says, "I have a difficult time getting into and then maintaining relationships because most men tell me that I am too independent for them and they feel like I don't need them." I love how the speaker first responds to her question. He first points out her body language while sitting in the room. He says, "I don't know how you are in relationships, but just by looking at you I can tell that you are very hard." He goes on to say more stuff that I have forgotten by now, but he was on point with his perception of her body language. When I looked in that woman's face, I could just sense that she had gone through so much pain and somewhere along the way she just continued to build a wall up to protect herself.

Now I'm not an expert in men and their needs, but one thing that I do know is that they want to feel like they are your protector and provider and if he ever senses that you don't need him for any of that then he will see his presence in your life as pointless. Well, this is how the real men that I've encountered think at least. And if this is the case, it makes sense why a woman such as herself had a difficult time keeping a man around. He felt unneeded because she was all things to herself, which left very little room for him.

I recall having another more up close and personal experience like this. A friend of mine was ready to get back on the dating scene, but all she did was go to work and go home, go to work and go home. So she and I, along with another friend, all decided to go out to this social networking event. I went more so for social support because I could have cared less if a guy talked to me that evening or not. But she did. So we got all dolled up and out the door we go. About an hour in, a few guys have already approached me and our other friend by this time, but none have approached her. One gentleman finally does come by to talk with her, but she was very short with him. Maybe she didn't like him. Who knows? But we are now a couple of hours in and she is over it and was just ready to go.

When we get back in the car, I asked her how she was feeling. I could tell that her hopes and expectations were not met that evening. She was open to an honest discussion so I pointed out to her that the entire time that we were there her body language said, "don't talk to me." I don't recall her smiling much, and she folded her arms most of the time. The whole time I was confused in my head because her words said that she wanted to be there, but I couldn't tell. I wanted to say, "if you want to be here then tell your face that because it didn't seem to get the memo." But I didn't say that because it wouldn't have been met with a warm welcome. She too, just like this other lady, had some seriously tough shells that were really great repellents for men.

The Fruit Tells it All

My heart went out to both of these ladies because I truly could relate. I use to be just like them. I was very tough on the outside, and it showed in my face and my body language. I promise it seemed like I use to always hear, "smile" from people that I would walk past. After hearing it for the millionth time I began to wonder, "what does my face and body language tell people?" It wasn't telling them that I was happy clearly!

I am very reflective, so I began to wonder how my heart issues could show up on my face and in my body language. I mean I was that woman that walked into a place and looked straight ahead and didn't make eye contact with anybody, and I didn't want to because I didn't want them to think that I was permitting them to talk to me. I just was not in a connecting mood often!

While reflecting, I thought of the scripture Luke 6: 43-45 *"For a good tree does not bear bad fruit, nor does a bad tree bear good fruit. [44] For every tree is known by its own fruit. For men do not gather figs from thorns, nor do they gather grapes from a bramble bush. [45] A good man out of the good treasure of his heart brings forth good; and an evil man out of the evil treasure of his heart brings forth evil. For out of the abundance of the heart his mouth speaks."* Then I flipped on over to read about the fruits of the spirit in Galatians 5:22-23. *"But the fruit of the Spirit is love, joy, peace, longsuffering, kindness, goodness, faithfulness, [23] gentleness, self-control."* Finally, I then read Proverbs 23:7a. *"For as he thinks in his heart, so is he."*

It's a Heart Thing

When you combine these scriptures, you begin to realize that we are the tree, our heart is the soil where the tree takes root, and our outward expressions are our fruit. A hard, decaying, or dead heart cannot produce any good fruit or any fruit at all. If joy, kindness, and gentleness were indicators of good fruit, then something was clearly wrong with my heart because I did not want to smile. Verse 45 says "out of the abundance of the heart his mouth speaks." I believe this verse applies so well to the stories I have shared because out of the abundance of our heart we will smile. Out of the abundance of our heart, we will frown. Out of the abundance of our heart, we will be warm and welcoming. Out of the abundance of our heart, we will be closed off, hard, and aloof. Whatever is in your heart will speak loud and clear nonverbally. They actually speak louder than your actual words. They don't just tell us who you are; they actually show us who you are and it will either draw us to you or push us away.

Your Femininity is so Attractive

I noticed that when I was super hard and felt that I needed to present myself as this superwoman tough lady, I would always attract very passive, weak, indecisive, and uncertain men. Now I don't mean weak as in he had puny muscles but weak in his ability to lead me. If it is true that opposites attract, I guess I was getting my opposite based on what I was showing externally. But my deep feminine nature would never be pleased with that type of man. No offense, but that sort of guy irritates me.

The more I became comfortable with being my feminine, gentle self, the more I'd start to attract very manly and dominate men. Which is what I am most attracted to. I even had one gentleman tell me that what he liked so much about me was how feminine I was. Now he was as manly as they can get and manly men are not attracted to manly women. Just think about a few of your friend's relationships. They most likely balance each other out on the feminine to masculine scale. If he is a ten-masculine-man, he probably has chosen a ten-feminine-woman. If he is a three-masculine-man, he probably has chosen a three-feminine-woman which means she probably is much more dominant and "manly" than he is.

To give you a visual, have you ever seen those huge body builder guys? If you were to see his preference in women, I'd bet it would also be a very fit woman but she'd most likely have your bikini fitness competition look and not so much of the bodybuilding competition look. If you don't know the difference, both have great strengths, but one just looks a little more feminine than the other. The bodybuilding competition women have much larger shredded muscles that look very much similar to the body of a male.

I could be wrong, but I highly doubt your big buff male will also choose a big buff woman. These are just my hypothesis but be observant and tell me what you notice. And observe yourself too. Single ladies, what type of men do you attract? The more masculine and dominant ones or the less masculine and more passive ones? Married ladies, what type of man did you marry? I'd be interested in knowing how you all's femininity and masculinity mesh in the relationship.

A Smile is Worth a Thousand Words

Let's go a little deeper into this femininity discussion. For starters, femininity is not about wearing pink every day with a tutu on! I don't own many pink items anyways so if that is what it is all about then I'd be in big trouble! Pink just doesn't look good on my skin tone, lol. I believe that femininity is all about a woman being loving, gentle, nurturing, and overall pleasant to be around. I can't tell you how many times a simple smile opened a door, helped to build a connection, or just simply made someone's day.

Here is an example. I go to the same gas station often, and the gentleman that works there once said, "I am so excited to see you when you come because you always smile at me, you are always nice to me, and you make my day because not many come in here happy." Another time I smiled and complimented this girl that worked at the YMCA. She was super tall so I told her that she belonged on the runway. That just lifted her spirits and she started walking down the hallway like it was a runway. I then had a client tell me that they chose me as a counselor because they liked my smile on my business card. I have gotten several free drinks at Starbucks because I was merely joyful with them. And I can go on and on about what a simple smile has done for me and has done for those that I come into contact with, but for me, I smile because I want to share Jesus with those that I encounter. Some share Him in different ways, but I share Him with a joyful smile.

Who Stole Your Smile?

I was at the cash register in a grocery store checking out and the woman hadn't cracked not one smile the entire time that I was standing in line, so when I get to her I try to make light conversation to see if she'd smile. She gave me a half-hearted smile by the time it was time for me to walk off. Before I walked off, I said to her, "you look so much better when you smile." I smiled at her and walked off.

When I got outside, I thought to myself, "I wonder who stole her smile from her?" What had happened to her for her to look so angry? If she and I were to sit down and have that conversation, I wouldn't be surprised to learn that it was an accumulation of events that slowly but surely took the joy right out of her life. I know that was the case for me at least. After being wounded in the same way over and over again, you lose the desire to care anymore. You lose the desire to be vulnerable and ultimately, all of those events end up hardening us and robbing us of one of our most powerful weapons, and that is our soft and gentle heart.

So who took your ability to be soft away? Who told you, directly or indirectly, that being feminine was not okay? I will say that I am all for women rising and taking back their power where they once felt oppressed. But what I am not here for is becoming a hard woman to prove my strength. Do I have to frown to show my strength? Do I have to flex my muscles to show my strength? Or, can I just put on a really pretty dress and my favorite pair of high heels and be considered strong? Can I not appreciate a man opening my door, pulling my chair out, walking with me on the inside of the sidewalk, and helping me carry the groceries in and still be considered strong? Do I have to bench press the same as a man to be considered strong? Can we be both feminine and strong? Can our femininity be our strength? I think so.

Now don't get it twisted, being feminine and gentle is not being weak. I am very much a type A dominating personality, but it is laced with femininity all over the place. I am very competitive and I like to conquer. Does that also make me little masculine? I'm sure my more "masculi traits come out when it comes to business, bu just have to know how to balance it and know to turn it on and off as needed. For examp probably don't need to bring your competitive/conquer attitude to your relationship and use it towards your partner. That just creates unnecessary tension. It's your gentle femininity that oozes from your inner beauty that commands his attention.

It's Your Inner Beauty

I believe that a woman's femininity is her inner beauty flowing out from her heart. You can be the ost attractive woman physically, but if you have gly inside then it just means you are pretty When your inner makeup matches your makeup then you, my friend, will be ot only will you be irresistible to those you will also be irresistible to God. re and open heart is much more n your skin tight jeans or your Samuel 16:7 He says, *"Do nce or at his physical ed him. For the Lord*

a
ne"
you
when
le, you

does not see as man sees; for man looks at the outward appearance, but the Lord looks at the heart."

Your open and receptive heart is what pleases God. Your ability to be trusting and vulnerable is also pleasing to God. It is in that secret and intimate place that He can truly reveal Himself to you as you reveal who you are to Him. Naked and unashamed.

I understand what it is like to know that God cares most about our internal beauty but to still wrestle with how you look externally. If you wrestle with and are insecure about your external appearance, then try asking the Lord to reveal to you all of the amazing things about your internal beauty. It as least worked for me. I was so insecure in many ways physically, but once God began to reveal to me the things that HE likes about me, all the other things that media likes to put a filter on or photoshop become less important to me. I began to desire to be much more beautiful internally than I did externally. And that is my hope for you as well; that you will begin to appreciate all of the things that make you beautiful internally and externally. It's not your booty or your beauty. It is your inner beauty, which is your spirit. It is your gentle feminine spirit that causes people to want to be close to you. Just think about it. Which would you prefer? A person that has a prickly porcupine hug or someone with a soft and fluffy hug? That soft and fluffy hug is synonyms to a nice and gentle spirit.

So what aspects of you are most people attracted to? Think long and hard about that question. Even ask those closest to you to be honest and tell you what they find most attractive and what they don't find as attractive. Be sure to ask people that are not just going to be negative but will give you constructive feedback. Sometimes we can be blindsided to our strengths and weaknesses, so I hope this one question helps you to self-reflect a little deeper.

Restored Joy

If you feel like your ability to smile and to be gentle have been stolen from you then it is my prayer that God would restore and heal those places in your life that need His special touch. I pray that God will help you to realize that your true strength lies in whom He made you to be and that is a woman with special abilities to captivate and touch a heart.

Add Double A Batteries to Your Gentleness

Before we wrap this topic of gentleness up, I wanted to be sure that I told you about the importance of adding the Double A's to your gentleness. The Double A's are assertiveness and aggressiveness. Yes, I know I just told you that your gentleness is your strength but there will be times when you need to be aggressively gentle. This does not mean going around with a frown on your face and beating up all men that pass you by so that you can get your point across. It basically means be who you are but never take no for an answer when God has already told you yes. I know the word aggressive sounds aggressive but take it to mean audacious and vigorous and not to mean hostility.

So remember these three things: (1) It will be your *aggression* that gets you in the right position, (2) It will be your *gentleness* that keeps you in the place, and (3) It will be your *assertiveness* that gets you what you want while in the place. Ruth effortlessly epitomizes this with the help of her "mentor" Naomi. Naomi coached Ruth on how to be gentle, assertive, and aggressive all in one. Let's looks at the story in Ruth 3. I will put a [G] to indicate her gentleness, an [AG] to indicate her aggressiveness and, an [AS] to indicate her assertiveness. The letters will follow the corresponding sentence (s).

"Therefore wash yourself and anoint yourself, put on your best garment and go down to the threshing floor; but do not make yourself known to

the man until he has finished eating and drinking. [G] *⁴ Then it shall be, when he lies down, that you shall notice the place where he lies; and you shall go in, uncover his feet, and lie down; and he will tell you what you should do." [G]*

⁵ And she said to her, "All that you say to me I will do."

⁶ So she went down to the threshing floor and did according to all that her mother-in-law instructed her. [AG] ⁷ And after Boaz had eaten and drunk, and his heart was cheerful, he went to lie down at the end of the heap of grain; and she came softly, uncovered his feet, and lay down. [G]

⁸ Now it happened at midnight that the man was startled, and turned himself; and there, a woman was lying at his feet. ⁹ And he said, "Who are you?"

So she answered, "I am Ruth, your maidservant. Take your maidservant under your wing, for you are a close relative." [AS]

¹⁰ Then he said, "Blessed are you of the Lord, my daughter! For you have shown more kindness at the end than at the beginning, in that you did not go after young men, whether poor or rich. [G] ¹¹ And now, my daughter, do not fear. I will do for you all that you request, for all the people of my town know that you are a virtuous woman. ¹² Now it is true that I am a close relative; however, there is a relative closer than I. ¹³ Stay this night, and in the morning it shall be that if he will perform the duty of a close relative for you—good; let him do it. But if he does not want to perform the duty for you, then I will perform the duty for you, as the Lord lives! Lie down until morning."

14 So she lay at his feet until morning, and she arose before one could recognize another. Then he said, "Do not let it be known that the woman came to the threshing floor." [AG] 15 Also he said, "Bring the shawl that is on you and hold it." And when she held it, he measured six ephahs of barley, and laid it on her. Then she went into the city." – Ruth 3:3-15

Ruth was aggressive. She was not supposed to be at the threshing floor but she had the audacity to be bold and bend the rules! That's what got her in the right place and the right position. Ruth was gentle. She softly walked to Boaz and uncovered his feet. She turned the aggression off and turned the gentleness on. She didn't make herself known until the evening. Now that is some self-control and calmness. We already know she smelled good and looked good so if she is anything like some of us ladies, she wanted him to see all of that greatness asap. But she knew she had to be subtle and that is what kept her in the room. Finally, Ruth was assertive. She basically proposed to Boaz. I'm not making this up. Go back and read verse 8. It wasn't called a "proposal" back then but if she was in our society today, she was down on one knee in this verse. He asked her who she was and she flat out told him who she was and what she wanted all in two sentences. And she didn't even ask, she told him to marry her. Now that is some next level assertive training. *[Side note: this is not your green light to go propose to some man.]*

I find it interesting that we talk about waiting for our Boaz but the scripture does not say that Boaz was looking for a wife. He saw her and immediately gave her favor. He fed her, gave her something to drink, and made her labor so much easier but his pursuit didn't seem to go beyond that. That was all fine and dandy but Naomi was like, "Sweetheart, dinner and a movie is nice and all but what you need is the ring so here is what you will do…(translated in modern day terms)." Truth be told, Naomi was the match-maker. Now yes, scripture says that he who finds a wife finds a good thing[1] but just because you find something doesn't mean you had to have been looking for it! I find money all of the time but I am never walking around saying, "I'm trying to find money." I just find it and then I say, "Wow, I just found some money" and I am just as blessed by the pleasant surprise!

If you remember nothing else from this chapter remember to be as gentle as a dove and as fierce as a roaring lioness when it comes time for it. And don't forget to pack your Double A's for the trip! I guarantee you that you will need them all. You may not need all three at the same time though so be sure that you know when to turn one on and one off. There may be times when your spouse just needs you to be gentle and there are times when he may desire for you to be aggressive and assertive in the relationship. Again, I am not referring to being hostile and quarrelsome. Here's a quick example. I did couples counseling with a young couple and the husband said, " I just wish that she would pursue me sometimes sexually. I just wish that she would initiate instead of it always being me." He wanted her lovely gentleness but he also wanted it to be blended with a little bit of spicy aggression. Remember that gentleness is your strength so if all else fails, you still have your heart.

Reflection Time

An irresistible woman is one who is calm and gentle. Her presence brings comfort not discord. An irresistible woman is able to smile at the days to come. She takes care of her outward beauty but she realizes that her true beauty lies within. An irresistible woman has a pure heart that is able to touch other hearts in a positive way. She realizes that her love IS her strength.

1. Has your smile ever been taken from you? What happened? How did you restore your smile? If your smile still hasn't been restored, simply ask the Lord to heal that broken place in your heart so that you can smile again.

2. What does it mean to have internal beauty? What type of "internal beauty products" do you use to make sure your insides are just as polished as your outsides? (For example, listening to my bible app truly helps me to polish my internal beauty. Scripture just has that

way of giving us a deep clean). That's just one example. What are some other ways?

3. Some people have different thoughts on the word "feminism", especially with the feminist movement. What does being feminine mean to you? How do you personally convey your femininity on a day-to-day basis?

CHAPTER THREE

Find Where You Are

Spiritual Seasons are Internal

It was a snowy day in Nashville, TN. As I was sitting in a rocking chair staring out of the window, I began to get emotional and joyful inside. I wasn't looking at anything in particular that was "joy evoking," I was just admiring the scenery. Some trees didn't have any leaves while others had beautiful yellow leaves that blew away with the wind.

The snow began to fall from gloomy grey clouds, and I found myself saying, "I am so happy!" I then rest in God's love for a moment, but then I think to myself that so many people could be doing the same thing and looking at the same stuff but experiencing a completely different emotion...such as depression, sadness, or loneliness.

It then dawned on me that your spiritual season is all about what is taking place on the inside of you. It is not determined by what is going on outside. So in reality, you have input, in part, to what your season will be. It doesn't matter what your surroundings look like, you can chose to have joy and peace regardless. I know what it is like to have our female hormones raging all over the place making our emotional choices much more difficult but will you look out the window and see the naked trees but still feel joy or will you look out the window and see the naked trees and experience great sadness and loneliness? It's your choice.

What Will Your Season Be?

If you are feeling a little dreary and gloomy in your current season, one way to change it is to change your perspective on the season. You can do this by learning what the season has to teach you so that you can get the lesson and become eligible to move on. Then there are times where you just have to wait the season out. But be of good cheer...seasons do change[1]. But, what do you do when the season doesn't seem to be changing and disappointments linger?

Dealing with Dissatisfaction

Going through a season of dissatisfaction can be by far the most uncomfortable, irritating, and frustrating thing to endure. We are often so engulfed in it that we have no idea how to find our way out. It can leave us feeling confused, lost, and even fearful of the unknown. But I discovered that if we could become much clearer about what is going on in our lives, we would feel less distraught and the feelings of powerlessness will begin to subside.

So I came up with a simple, 7-step process to deal with dissatisfaction:

1. Identify what is causing you dissatisfaction. Be specific.
2. What is it about the situation that is causing you to feel dissatisfied? Be specific.
3. What are your core feelings that are present? (Google: "feelings wheel" if you need some help with feelings words. It's the rainbow circle one that has mad, scared, joyful, powerful, peaceful, and sad at the center.)
4. Having feelings is not bad but how we handle them can be negative. Are your emotions causing you to feel weakened, burdened, or negative in any way OR are your emotions simply helping to guide you to reveal what you

need? For example, when I am angry I have a choice: (a) let my anger control me and paralyze me or (b) channel my anger to fuel my passion. Here's another example. When I am anxious, I can choose to (a) allow my anxiety to take over and run my thoughts or (b) use my anxiety to help me realize that I simply need clarity and reassurance.

5. Identify specifically what your feeling has been trying to tell you (ask the Holy Spirit to help you with insight). If your emotions could talk and explain to you exactly what is going on, what would they say? (i.e., maybe your sadness will say "I'm hurting, and I need you to pay attention to what you have been trying to ignore.)

6. Ask the Holy Spirit to help you understand what you are feeling. Listen to what He has to say.

7. Create a plan, now, on how you will combine the information that you received in #5 and #6 and make the necessary changes.

I was looking through my old journals, and I found what I wrote when going through these same seven steps about two years ago. Here is a brief paragraph example:

I am dissatisfied with being single. I feel that I have been faithful to the Lord and I feel that I have been trying to do everything right, so I just don't understand why I am still in the waiting season. This makes me feel very frustrated, lonely, angry, anxious, and embarrassed. Each of these feelings makes me feel burdened and confused. There are times, though, when I can just take all of these emotions and channel them to my writing or work; and that is a good thing. Another good thing is that when I am lonely, I sometimes find myself wanting to serve others and this makes me feel better too. My frustration, anger, and anxiety have been trying to tell me that I am not in control but God is, and I should learn to be comfortable with that. My embarrassment has been trying to tell me that I care way too much about how other people perceive me. It doesn't matter what they think of me, and I am not less of a woman if I am single. It is also telling me that I have been comparing myself to others and that is not healthy. My loneliness has been trying to tell me that I desire connectivity with other people. Yes for a spouse, but at times, also for God and for friendship. Ultimately, the Holy Spirit is saying that He designed me to have relationships with others. I have a huge heart, and I desire to love. There is nothing wrong with desiring connectivity. I simply need to refocus my attention from getting a husband to building my relationship with God, who is my first Husband. As I draw closer to

Him, everything else falls into my peripheral vision, and it will be less on the forefront of my mind. And ultimately, I just need to trust His timing.

Ok, now it is your turn. I combined some of my emotions for the sake of time here, but I want you to elaborate on each emotion. This will take some time to go through each feeling that you are feeling, but it is worth every minute of it!

Trust His Timing

God has told me to trust His timing a lot; as I am sure He has told you. But what do you do when your timing and His timing do not seem to line up quite as you'd like? I mean, if it were up to me, my time would always be NOW! But we know that God doesn't always operate that way.

So, my credit card company gave me a great lesson on timing. I had to pay my bill that day, or otherwise, I would have received a late fee. I ended up calling around 11:50 PM (Central Time Zone) but when I called, the lady told me I was still late because the cut off time was 11:59 PM (Eastern Time Zone) the day that the bill is due. To me, I was early but to her (being an hour ahead) I was late.

What determined whether I was late or on time was not based on where I was but was based on her location. I didn't get mad because I understood the policy, plus she showed favor and still did not charge the late fee, but this got my mind churning about how God's timing works.

He doesn't run on an Eastern, Central, Mountain, or Pacific Time Zone. He runs on His timing, GST-God's Standard Time. ☺ Many times this becomes difficult for us while we are in the waiting seasons. We feel that God is taking too long to show up because according to "our time," He is late. However, God is not looking at our earthly time to determine when He will make adjustments in our life. According to His timing, He will be right on time. And regardless if we feel He has shown up late or even early, it will always be perfect timing.

Your timing and due dates will not persuade God one way or the other, so it is in our best interest to just trust in Him and rely on His perfect timing. Just like with my bill, in actuality I was late, but she made it appear as if I was on time. God may show up "seemingly late" but even in those moments...He is still on time!

Think about it like your doctor's appointment. They give you a set time of when to arrive at the doctor's office, but there is no guarantee that you will be seen promptly @ 8:30 AM. The doctor may see you right on time, or she may see you 30 minutes past that time, BUT one thing you can hold firm to is that the doctor WILL see you, you just have to show up and be patient.

Or, think about it from a pregnant woman's perspective. The doctor gives her a due date of when to expect her baby to be born. Rarely have I seen a baby born on that exact date though. I think it is given more so for a guesstimated arrival time frame based on when she got pregant. The parents are beginning to prepare for his/her arrival well in advance so that regardless if the baby comes out earlier or later than expected, they will be ready. Just because the baby does not come out when you expect it, does not mean it is not coming out. TRUST me, that little one has to come out sooner or later if he/she wants to or not.

When that DUE time comes, there is no stopping it from coming and just like that baby, we all have an appointed time! Just show up and be ready when your name is called. And while waiting, read Habakkuk 2:3 if you need a little encouragement. *"For the vision is yet for an appointed time; but at the end it will speak, and it will not lie. Though it tarries, wait for it; because it will surely come, it will not tarry."* Also read Genesis 18:14 and Exodus 9:5 for additional reading.

What God has promised you will surely come! His word will not return to Him void so it WILL happen[2]! Whatever your IT is. If He said it then so shall it be. Stop wondering IF it will happen and start believing that it WILL happen. If God has given you a promise, then you can take it to the bank so start preparing for whatever it is that He has promised you. It will come sooner than later.

How Soon is Soon!?

I know that some of you have been waiting for a long time already and you are probably thinking the same way I did, and that was, "if ONE more person tells me to wait and trust God!" You know that place you get to and say, "ok God I know you are going to do it because you told me a million times but you keep saying soon so how soon is soon?" I got tired of being TOLD over and over what was to come I simply wanted to SEE it. Have you ever been in one of these types of situations?

I have, one too many times. I recall standing in my kitchen one day just so confused about what God was doing. I stood there asking several questions like, "Where am I?", "Is my life still pleasing to you?", "What season am I in?", and "Why do I feel confused about what is going on?"

I figured if I were in a "winter" (isolation) season it would help me understand a little bit more but He didn't tell me what season I was in. He instead had me finish watching a sermon by Bishop T.D. Jakes. I watched the entire sermon and was still confused as to what God was trying to tell me. Bishop had finished preaching, but He was still ministering to the people and getting ready to pray, so I decided to watch it all to the very end.

As I was listening to his final comments, I began to cry because it was in those final words that God spoke to me through Bishop and helped me to understand what was going on in my life. Every word that Bishop said at the end spoke directly to all of my internal struggles!

Here is what Bishop Jakes said in a sermon titled Work Your Faith Part II (Posted Oct 18, 2013- see the link in the chapter notes to watch[3].

> *"So the Lord sent this message as a location mechanism for you to understand where you are...you think that the enemy is attacking you. You think you are going through spiritual warfare. But this is not the enemy, and this is not spiritual warfare. This is God taking what you heard and what you believed, and He is mixing it together.*
> *The Lord told me to tell you...you are not lost, you are not in trouble,*

the enemy is not winning. Let me tell you where you are...you're in the mix! "

Maybe this is the same place that you are in. You've believed and sought God for a particular thing, and it seems like you are moving farther away from and not towards what He promised. It is just the mixing process, and it feels like one because you seem to be going round and round in circles, but all He is doing is taking His promises and your faith and blending them together to produce the final outcome.

The mixing and baking process is never fun while you are going through because it can be uncomfortable and it requires a waiting period, BUT it is very necessary! So how soon is soon?! Think about it from a baking perspective. How soon can you eat a piece of your pound cake in the oven? As soon as it is done. Waiting can be weary but may your mind now find peace with this new revelation into your situation. Remind yourself often that *"those who wait on the Lord shall renew their strength; They shall mount up with wings like eagles, They shall run and not be weary, They shall walk and not faint[4]."*

This verse says that those who wait on the Lord shall renew their strength. So maybe, just maybe, if you are worn out and weary it may be a sign that you are waiting on the wrong thing. Instead of waiting for a man...wait on the Lord. Instead of waiting on your husband to act right...wait on the Lord. Instead of waiting for _____....wait on the Lord. Why? Because He said that *"[He] will keep him in perfect peace, whose mind is stayed on [Him], because he trusts in [Him][5]."* While you are waiting just know that it can happen any day now.

I know that some of us can go from one extreme to the next so if someone says "don't' think about it" then they will do whatever it takes to distract themselves. That is not what I am asking you to do.

Don't be distraction focused, be destiny focused. You don't have to consume hours of your favorite show just to keep your mind preoccupied. That's a waste of time. Instead, focus on God and where He has you right now.

Stop Focusing on What's Next and Focus on What's Now

In my book, *Internal Navigator*, I talk about how the Holy Spirit guides us as we are in route to our destiny. I correlate the Holy Spirit to a navigational system, and I talk about how they both have similar features.

One thing that I mention is how a navigational system does not continue to give you new instructions if you have yet to complete the first step it gave you. When you are on a long trip, it will tell you to remain on the expressway for X amount of miles, and you may not hear its voice for another hour.

Just like the navigational system, the Holy Spirit will not waste His breath telling you to do something else when you have yet to fulfill the first step. Our steps are ordered by the Lord, which means one step will lead us to the next step and so on[6].

If you are in a place where you are asking God what is next but He does not seem to be responding then maybe you should rephrase your question and ask, "Lord, what should I be doing NOW?" instead of, "Lord, what should I do NEXT?" He probably has already given you something that you could be doing so He is waiting on you to do that first before He gives you anything new.

I found this to be true while writing my first book. I wanted God to give me the first, middle, and last steps because I am a planner who wants to know how things will flow. So this new idea of doing the first set of instructions before getting the next set just burst my bubble because I wanted to know it all up front. He would just tell me to write. And I did. Then, as I got to the final chapters in the book He then began giving me new instructions on what to do next with the finished product. It wasn't until I did what I was first told to do that He then was able to progress me forward.

Are there areas in your life that seem to be at a standstill and you feel it should be further along than what it is? Is the delay due to you? Could your focus be off? Re-evaluate what you are doing and ask God to reveal to you the steps that you have been attempting to overlook and skip past. Every step with God has purpose and meaning behind it[7]. So before He gives you the promise, can He trust you with the process?

Tested to be Trusted

Back in 2012, I had three consecutive dreams all in one night that were dealing with the same things;

faith and trust. In the first dream, I was going around trying to figure out why one particular lady was given such a great amount of trust from God. I didn't understand why but I said, "Well soon the next person will have it too." The second dream was me just talking to a friend about the first dream, and a website of some sort was mentioned. Finally, the third dream was the same thing, but the website was mentioned a little more in detail and something about silver. II Timothy was added here too.

As I re-read these dreams in my journal and reflected on them, I soon realized that this woman that I was searching for in the first dream was me and the whole discussion about faith & trust provided me insight into the season that I was in at the time.

During that time in my life, my faith was truly being pressed, pulled, and strained. My level of trust and dependence in God had been exposed, and my level of strength and endurance was tested. You never know your level of faith, trust, and strength until you are put into a predicament where they are needed.

I had the dreams several months before my intense test that challenged my own faith and trust in God. I can reflect back many years later and say that I did indeed pass the test. I said I trusted God BEFORE the test, but He had to see if I truly meant it. Yea, I meant it when everything was cookies and ice cream, but the truth really comes out when you are put through the test of fire. That experience allowed me to see that God gives great trust to those who have been tested and have endured without neglecting Him; to those who kept the faith.

One thing about the first dream that I love is when I said, "Well soon the next person will have it too." Keep in mind that you are not going through just for you. So many people's blessings and deliverances are attached to you! When you come out, they come out too! So you must endure the test even when it hurts.

Yes, going through hurts but I have learned to look at the bigger picture! I have learned that 1) God trusts me enough to go through and come out, 2) my ability to endure and persevere is a necessity because others are depending on me, 3) simply put, I am so much better because of it, and 4) I have been able to know God for myself on a deeper level than before!

I don't know about you, but I want ALL that God has for me! ALL of it! So if I have to be tested, so be it. If I have to be pruned, so be it. If I have to cry, so be it. If I have to yell, so be it. If I have to fight, so be it. If I have to wait, so be it. I am getting my stuff at any cost!

The promise doesn't come without a test of faith and trust first. You will be tested to see if you are just all talk or if you got some walk in you too. And you will be tested to see just how much you actually do believe. The enemy doesn't want to just let you have it so he will fight you tooth and nail to try and hinder you from getting it.

Before God gives you the weight of your promise, He needs to know if He can trust you with it. Soon you will find out, and that is reason for the test! Fight the good fight, keep the faith, persevere, and get what God has for you! Don't be afraid when put in the "batting cage" of life to test your swing to see what you got. Remember, it's only a test! Read these scriptures for further encouragement: Romans 5:1-5; II Timothy 2:1-3; 4:4-8.

Take some time to look over your life and recap all of the lessons that you have learned through people and circumstances in life. Take those lessons, learn from them, and help somebody that follows behind you. And most importantly, finish the course (test) so that you can graduate to the next level. You can be your biggest hindrance from moving up a level if you do not do the work at your current level.

Reflection Time

An irresistible woman knows how to minimize distractions and focus on what is most important. She is a discerner of time and she doesn't waste time. She knows where she is and trust's God no matter what season she is in. She does not grow weary in well doing or in waiting because her focus is on the Lord. An irresistible woman can be trusted with precious eternal treasures.

1. Think about the current season that you are in. Where does most of your time, energy, and focus go? Are there areas where you need to shift focuses? Explain.
2. How do you handle being told to wait?
3. *"The Lord had said to Abram, "Leave your country, your people and your father's household and go to the land I will show you."* – Genesis 12:1. Take note of how God said go to a place I will show you. He told Him to go but didn't tell Him where until he did the first

step of going. How teachable are you from God's perspective? Would He say you are a good listener? Would He say you require a lot of micromanaging? Would He say that He trusts you to do what He has asked?

4. Is your character and your behaviors as you go through your tests showing God that He can truly trust you with the promise? Or, is your character and your behaviors showing Him that you can be a bit unstable and unpredictable at times?

5. What tests do you continue to fail and why? (To know what tests you continue to fail look at the pattern of the same situations you find yourself in...there is something you have yet to learn so you will continue to go through until you learn it).

CHAPTER FOUR

Find What It's All About

It's Not About You

I remember like it was yesterday. I was in Brentwood, TN driving down the winding Concord Road at night. My eyes filled with uncontrollable tears, and my heart was experiencing, what felt like unbearable pain. I was on a rollercoaster ride of emotions feeling both sad and angry. "It just doesn't make sense," I tell my mom on the phone. "Why is it that every time I fall in love with a guy that I actually want and invest so much time and energy in he leaves? I mean, I thought this guy was my husband, and he made it seem like he truly cared for me too!"

My mom, being the awesome, caring mom that she is tried to help by giving me some encouragement. She said, "well maybe God is just trying to teach you something." That thought had crossed my mind but hearing it again only made me angrier, and I said, "Well what is the lesson!? I have been doing everything God has asked me to do! Why won't He just tell me what He wants me to do? I promise I will do it. I don't need another heartbreak to teach me a lesson. If He would just tell me the lesson, I will do it!"

I was so upset and sad that we just end the call so I could gather myself. I'm still driving and crying, and in the background, a song is playing, and I hear the lyrics, "just breathe..." by Jonny Diaz.

God follows up with a whisper and says, "Breathe." I fill my lungs with air, and I let it out. God then says, "This is not about you, and it keeps hurting because you keep taking it personally." "Wait, God what do you mean I am taking it personally? This has happened to me, so that is why I am personally hurt," I say back.

He goes on to explain to me that just because He allows a man in my life, does not mean I am supposed to fall in love. He said that He was using me to help them. I actually didn't like the sound of that. In my mind, I was thinking how I didn't want to be used in that way, and I didn't want to have my heart broke just so that the guy could gain something while I feel like I lost something. Here is the moment when God had to teach me how to guard my heart and to discern whether a guy had just come temporarily or if he would be around a lot longer. At first, it was difficult, but when my perspective changed about what God was actually doing, it became much easier. No longer would I just fall head over hills; I was able to freely give friendship and freely receive it without planning our wedding in my head on the second date.

Clarity Brings the Calm

I had much more clarity about this particular area in my life after a few ah-ha moments that helped me get the point. One, in particular, was a conversation with my mom's friend. It's so great when you have a whole team of prayer warriors and people who hear from God and can help bring clarity to your circumstances. I remember getting a call from her while I was sitting in Target parking lot. I honestly didn't want to answer because I didn't want to hear another, "just be patient, the Lord has a special husband just for you, and he's going to me amazing!" "Yes, I know he is going to be amazing, so where is he?!" is what I would think when people would say that.

But the way she broke it down made so much sense. I am a visual learner, so her example literally gave me a paradigm shift. So here is how she explained what was going on.

> *Imagine that God told you that He had a brand new computer that He wanted to give you. I mean it had all the bells and whistles on it. It is the latest of the latest in technology. But imagine Him saying, it is being manufactured so I can't give it to you just yet, but if you don't feel like waiting, you can just take the current computer that is out. He presents you with a choice. I mean a computer has been on your wish list for so long so taking the current model sounds very intriguing. I mean at least you have a form of what you wanted; even if it is not the latest and greatest.*

But, you suck it up and are willing to have delayed gratification, so you tell God, yes, you will wait for the newest computer to come out. He says ok great and then says, "While you are waiting on your computer, I am going to bring different people into your life who I want you to help prepare for their computers too." Now you have another choice. You can be salty and selfish and refuse to help other's get their computers OR you can choose to be cooperative because ultimately you realize that as you are helping them prepare for their computer, you are also gaining the necessary wisdom and knowledge that you will also need when your computer arrives. So you help one person prepare for his computer and the moment he moves on from you he gets his computer. And this happens over and over again until you are thinking, "Ok wait a minute God, I am helping all these people get their computers but where is mine." And God reminds you, "It is being manufactured. It is being prepared. It is one of a kind. A rare commodity that will make your entire wait worth it. This kind takes more time." So you find peace once again knowing that He will withhold no good thing from you[1].

When I Help You, I Help Me

This computer metaphor truly helps you to see how you can "kill two birds with one stone." As you are interacting with the opposite sex, you begin to realize the areas of your heart, mind, and habits that can use some tweaking and change. You don't know how "coo-coo," for lack of better terms, or unstable you are until you are challenged by someone who has your heart. My female friends just do not bring up the same heart issues as my male friends would. Am I saying just to go out and start dating everybody so that you can learn all that you need to learn before you get married? Nope, I am not saying that. But I will say that God did grace me in different seasons of my life to date and be in a relationship, and there were also times when He wanted me to be single. Consult God with what you should do.

But I honestly think that had I got married before I learned certain lessons or dealt with certain heart issues or mindsets, I may have already been divorced or miserably married. The only reason I say that is because I use to be so stubborn, set in my own ways, viewed men more as an accessory rather than a necessity, didn't know when just to shut up because I always had something to say smart, and I would chunk you the deuces in the minute. I mean my patience and tolerance level was at a negative 25 so my level of work-it-out-ness was almost nonexistent. Remember Sweet Brown from the news? My favorite phrase used to be, and still is in some areas, "Ain't nobody got time for that!"

How I behaved, how I thought, and how I felt were NOT conducive to a healthy marriage. The list could have gone on a little longer, but you get the point. I wasn't ready and had God given me a husband back then I would have ruined it all by myself. The enemy wouldn't even have to lift a finger to try to destroy what God put together. I would've dropped that fancy, state of the art "computer" in a heartbeat. I would have been so careless with it.

I'm just being honest, and I believe if a lot more of us would just be honest with ourselves we will move much quicker towards being ready to have our own "computers" too. And I believe we'd stop destroying and pushing away what God actually sends to us. You better thank God He didn't send you a blessing before you were ready for it. I know

I am; even if I did kick and scream out of impatience. The moment I realized that it wasn't about me and the moment I was willing to actually help someone else along the way is when I had the greatest sense of clarity about my role in that particular season. As I was helping others to become prepared, I was being prepared myself.

Reflection Time

An irresistible woman is one who has clearly prepared for what she believes to come. She demonstrates her faith by her diligence in preparation. She commands her flesh to submit and demands that her desires align with the will of God. She understands that delayed gratification is better than impatient settling. An irresistible woman is self-aware and honest with herself and with others. She is not selfish but selfless. An irresistible woman is willing to help and serve others even if it doesn't benefit her. She doesn't just take; she knows how to give. No matter what, she is consistent; even when what is asked of her seems to be an inconvenience. People trust her because they know she will be consistent and reliable.

1. Write down some of your most important lessons you have learned from previous friendships and relationships. How will those lessons help you in future relationships?

2. Talk about your experience with delayed gratification? Do you find yourself giving in to what is most convenient and assessable to you in the moment or are you able to wait for what is best for you?

3. When it comes to your personal and relational life, what are some things that you are unclear about and need clarity on? Write them down and ask the Lord to begin to make things clearer for you.

CHAPTER FIVE

Find Your Heart

Stop Killing Your Own Heart

One Sunday morning God showed me a picture of a woman gripping for dear life to her heart. That woman was me. I recall praying intensely for my heart and the hearts of those closest to me a couple of years ago. On this particular Sunday, God revealed to me the condition of my heart, and I was utterly oblivious to what He showed me. I was under the assumption that my emotional heart was in good condition, but unbeknownst to me, it wasn't.

He showed me how I had put a grip so tight on my heart to the point of suffocation. Imagine squeezing a stress ball as hard as you can. That's the image I had with my heart. He told me that I was holding onto my heart so tight out of fear of giving it to anyone. In my mind, I was protecting and guarding it, but I was doing more harm than help. I was unknowingly killing my own heart all because of fear of it being broke again. The timing of this conversation with God gets even more interesting when you realize this was back in 2015 when I had first published my second book titled *The Caged in Heart: How Your Childhood Wounds are Affecting Your Adult Life*.

I talk on and on about how to realize if you have a caged heart and how to set it free if so. So how could it be? How could "the caged in heart" lady be the one with a suffocating heart?! Well, I finally was able to free my heart from the cage that all my painful relationship experiences put it in. And because it was finally free from bondage and stitched up real nice, I got to a place where I refused to let it go back behind the walls that I once had built to protect it. So it was free but I had a death grip on it.

I'd correlate this to a mother who is super watchful and antsy about every little movement her child makes after finally healing from a broken bone. You just don't want them to get hurt again so even the slightest jump off a stump or an invite outside to play can put you slightly on the nervous edge.

Self-Imprisonment

I was that parent. Afraid to let my heart go out and play again. I felt that inside and close to me was the safest place for it to be. Now, instead of it being in the cage that the men put it in, I now had it in the palm of my hand with an unwilling grip to even open up slightly to love and be loved! I quickly realized, when you try to block the bad from coming in you are also preventing the good from coming in or going out. So not only was I blocking the hurt; I did a great job at that. But I was also prohibiting love, joy, and connecting from coming in or flowing out. You can't block one without blocking the other. My pain caused me to go from one extreme to the other. I was doing the very thing to my heart that I didn't want someone else to do, which was hurting it!

Numb but Still Hurting

So instead of recklessly loving like I use to, I became numb to even loving at all. I became very nonchalant and truly did not care who came or left (as it relates to men)! That's not me. I developed selfish/conditional love because I poured out so much and found myself empty. Because I gave so much only to get so little in return, I decided that I needed to know AHEAD of time "what's in it for me?!" This attitude and mindset left zero room for allowing things naturally to grow and flow.

I became increasingly numb with this mindset. Growing numb was a defense mechanism. It protected me from feeling the hurt and it got the job done similarly to what callous does to dancer's feet, and weight trainers or athlete's hands. With enough damage to that same area, your skin naturally builds a callous. And over time, what use to hurt you no longer does. For these professions, callous sounds like an advantage. You can still use your hands and feet over and over again without feeling the pain. BUT, callous is not an advantage when it comes to your heart. Using a heart that does not feel is basically being heartless. And we all know the damage a heartless person can bring to oneself and others.

Now, when I hear a woman, who appears to be very tough on the outside, say, "I don't care anymore, it doesn't bother me, I'm numb to it, it doesn't matter, etc." I know that deep down inside, beneath all the callous, she is probably a wounded woman who needs special attention and care to truly mend her bleeding heart that she is probably unaware is still bleeding. The thing about internal bleedings is that you can't see them so you can be bleeding internally and slowly but surely losing life. But, isn't it like God to never let us sit and die unnecessarily?

Heart Check-up

God cares so much about our hearts that He will do what it takes to get our attention and give us life. So, after He gave me a face-to-face talk about my suffocating heart, He then followed it up with two sermons, one friend, and one song telling me the EXACT same thing.

On this same Sunday, I streamed online and watched Bishop T.D. Jakes preach from the subject, "Heart Attack," and that was just a double whopper confirmation of the image God showed me earlier that morning!! Then I went to church at Mount Zion in Nashville, and Bishop Walker talked about "What You've Been Waiting on is About to Happen." Both of these sermons revealed to me that I had hardened my heart. I had anesthetized my own heart to avoid any further hurt and disappointment. I had become the pro at numbing and shrugging my shoulders saying, "hmm who cares!" or "whatever, I've heard that before!" Those sermons were heart check-ups number two and three.

Then my friend was essentially saying the same things to me as well, so that was checkup number four. But THEN on Monday, I got heart checkup number five that brought it all full circle. I was playing music on YouTube as I was getting ready to go to my prayer closet to spend time with God to deal with my heart issues and this random song that I never heard came on. It is called "Tell Your Heart to Beat Again" by Danny Gokey. At first, it was just background noise, so I wasn't listening to it until those simple words..."tell your heart to beat again"...rang in my spirit and I immediately started to cry! It struck a chord with my heart once again! It was like a defibrillator to my heart. I had confirmation after confirmation after confirmation that I literally was killing my heart ALL ON MY OWN!! Forget another man "breaking it" I was KILLING IT!! In all of this, God was saying CLEAR...SHOCK! Trillion let your heart LIVE again!

I know some of you may have concerns about "living again." Some of you may be saying, "that's too scary, I'm afraid, what if I get hurt again, what if this, what if that?!" Trust me, I've been down that scary "what if" road and while I may not have answers for all of your "what if's" I do know that there is still life after pain, so please, tell your heart it is okay to live again!

You Need Your Heart and So Does God

Although I was the "caged in heart" book lady, I realized that I was just a wounded healer who had to continue to do a "heart check" too! So allow me to encourage you as I encouraged myself. Don't let your experiences change you. I use to give love so freely not expecting anything in return, but my past pains tried to take that gift away from me. As you can imagine, with the ministry and calling on my life, I CAN'T HAVE A DEAD HEART!! EVERYTHING that I do and talk about has to do with our HEART!

God created me with a HUGE heart! I love people to pieces! I love insanely quickly. I see the good even when others may see nothing but negative, but I began to question if something was wrong with me. I thought, "how could you love so easily and so quickly! Surely you are way too emotional!" But, one of my lovely friends simply reframed it for me and said, "there is nothing wrong with your heart, you are just like God and love to love, and you do it quickly just like Him." So for those of you who have that gallon kind of love, it's ok, you just have a lot of love to go around, so don't ever stop loving!

Guard Your Heart

Some of you have probably been waiting on the verse that tells us to guard our hearts. It reads, *"Above all else, guard your heart, for everything you do flows from it."* Yes, I wrestled with this verse after God told me I was suffocating my heart. My rebuttal was, "well I'm just guarding it as you told us to." He gently burst that bubble by giving me an amazing Bible lesson on this verse. So here is a brief recap of what He showed me in the scripture.

He had me to read Proverbs 4:23, which is the one above, but then He instructed me to now start at verse one and read all the way to the end. I encourage you to do the same but here are some of the verses:

Verses 4-8 (NIV)

"Then he taught me, and he said to me,
"Take hold of my words with all your heart;
keep my commands, and you will live.
[5] *Get wisdom, get understanding;*
do not forget my words or turn away from them.
[6] *Do not forsake wisdom, and she will protect you;*
love her, and she will watch over you.
[7] *The beginning of wisdom is this: Get wisdom.*
Though it cost all you have, get understanding."

Ok so here we are told to put His words of wisdom in our hearts and wisdom will protect us.

Then verses 11-13 (NIV) says:

"I instruct you in the way of wisdom and lead you along straight paths.
[12] *When you walk, your steps will not be hampered; when you run, you will not stumble.*
[13] *Hold on to instruction, do not let it go;*
guard it well, for it is your life."

Here we are told to hold tight to the instructions given because it will guard and save our lives.

Keep reading. Ok, now we are at verses 20-23 (NIV):

> *"My son, pay attention to what I say;*
> *turn your ear to my words.*
> [21] *Do not let them out of your sight,*
> *keep them within your heart;*
> [22] *for they are life to those who find them*
> *and health to one's whole body.*
> [23] *Above all else, guard your heart,*
> *for everything you do flows from it."*

Are you clearly seeing this now? It is God's words, His instructions, and His wisdom that we listen to and keep in our hearts that guards our heart!

You don't have to suffocate your heart or keep it in a cage to guard it! Simply use wisdom when it comes to the affairs of your heart. Not only will wisdom guard your heart but so will Peace! Philippians 4:7 says *"and the peace of God, which surpasses all understanding, will guard your hearts and minds through Christ Jesus."* When you make wise decisions, you have peace, and when you have peace and wisdom you have the ultimate heart guard!

And to put the icing on the cake, God wrapped up this bible lesson with me by saying, "I am your defender and your protector, not you!" Psalm 119:114 says, *"You are my hiding place and my shield; I hope in your word."* And other translations have used the words defender and protector. I also needed to hear this because I trusted my heart in my hand more so than I did in His hand. I had become a little 'g' god to my heart. That's no Bueno! No good at all!

So all in all, guarding your heart is pretty much a lightweight job for you. God, Wisdom, Peace, and Instructions are your S.W.A.T. team. But the question is, are you USING them?! I actually spend an entire chapter talking about this in my book *"Owning Possible."* The chapter is titled, "Develop Your Foresight" and it's all about how to make wisdom and warning signs work for your good.

Spoiler alert though; they only work if you pay attention to them.

A Few Steps to Set Your Heart Free

If you connected with anything I've said in this chapter then here are just a few things you can do to begin to set your heart free:

- Forget about yesterday and move on!
- Relinquish control over your life and heart to God
- Learn to deal with ambiguity
- Don't worry about "what if"
- Learn to Trust God 100%
- Know that all things are working for your good

The ultimate goal is to open your hands and let your heart be free!

Reflection Time

An irresistible woman has both clarity of heart and mind. No matter what season she is in, she is emotionally and mentally stable. She does not allow negative experiences to change her at her core. She understands that she is love and that she must continue to be the light for those around her. She does not waste time holding onto things; she simply knows how to forgive and let go. She continues to challenge her heart to be more like Christ's and she has learned to fully yield her heart to the Lord. An irresistible woman is one who has dealt with her past baggage. She doesn't come to the table with bags and bags of luggage. She knows how to give love freely and how to receive it just as freely. An irresistible woman is one not controlled by her past, but she has taken responsibility for her own reactions to what happened to her. An irresistible woman is free in her heart, and you can see it through her smile.

1. Guarding my heart God's way feels impossible because I feel/think that _____ .

2. God, Wisdom, Peace, and Instructions will do a way better job of guarding your heart than you will. Talk about your ease or difficulty in letting each guard your heart vs. you.

3. What if your "what if's" never happen? Calculate how much time, energy, and focus you would have wasted?

Dear *She's Possible Sister*,

I implore you to **Be Confident**.

Go the extra mile to have **Clarity of heart and mind**.

And show up and **Be Consistent** in every area of your life.

When you do, you will then be...

...**Unstoppable,**

...**Irresistible,** and

...**Possible**!

What can stop a confident woman who knows who she is and where she is going?

Who can resist a woman who has a heart of gold?

What is impossible for a woman who is guarded, guided, and protected by God?

The answers are NOTHING, NOONE, and NOTHING!!

So what's holding you back? In my book titled *"Owning Possible"*, I state that the impossible becomes possible when you own it. IMPOSSIBLE becomes I'm POSSIBLE when you know who you are! You have much to do so figure out who you are quickly, take responsibility for the condition of your heart and mind, and work the gifts that God has placed deep down inside of you. You have all that you need to make your wildest dreams a reality so arise woman! Arise, and let's make it happen!

Love Always,

Trillion Small

Your *She's Possible Sister*

Chapter Notes

Introduction
1. https://en.oxforddictionaries.com/definition/irresistible

Chapter One
1. Moana. Disney Movie (2016). Soundtrack, *Know Who You Are* by Auli'l Cravalho http://movies.disney.com/moana
2. Genesis 29:31-35
3. Genesis 32:22-30
4. Luke 8:43-48

Chapter Two
1. Proverbs 18:22

Chapter Three
1. Ecclesiastes 3:1
2. Isaiah 55:11
3. Work Your Faith Part II .Posted Oct 18, 2013. Retrieved from https://www.youtube.com/watch?v=eFnH71QEB8c
4. Isaiah 40: 31
5. Isaiah 26:3
6. Psalm 37:23
7. Psalm 37:23; Proverbs 20:24; Jeremiah 10:23

Chapter Four
1. Psalm 84:11

Chapter Five
1. Proverbs 4:23 (NIV)

About the Author

Dr. Trillion Small has a Ph.D. in Clinical Counseling and is a Licensed Marriage and Family Therapist. She is a TEDx Speaker. Her talk, which can be found on Youtube, is titled "Overcoming the Fear of Love". She is also the Founder/Lead Organizer for TEDxFrisco in Frisco, Texas. Additionally, Dr. Small is a certified John Maxwell coach. She is the author of several books and is the Founder/CEO of They Speak Publishing.

Dr. Small is passionate about youth development. She is the Executive Director for the 501(c)(3) Prepare Academy. Their focus is to personally and professionally prepare the next generation and equip the community to be emotionally & relationally intelligent.

She was honored and recognized as Nashville's 2016 Black 40 under 40 and has been seen on national and international television and heard on several local news and nationally syndicated talk show radio stations such as CBS, NBC, The Word Network, American Family Radio, Total Living Network and more.

YOUR GUIDE TO MAKING THE
IMPOSSIBLE POSSIBLE!

Owning Possible

DR. TRILLION SMALL, LMFT

Order *Owning Possible* on Amazon

The impossible is possible when you own it! Fear, doubt, low confidence, and unbelief won't stand a chance against the fight for your potential. It is time for you to take ownership of all that is possible in your life.

Consider "Owning Possible" your plan to discovering all that is possible as you remove the greatest barrier that keeps you away from being all that you can be and having all that you can have. In "Owning Possible" Trillion Small shares several practical tools to help guide you as you eliminate these barriers and reveal what was already inside of you! There are possibilities out there with your name on it; let's get up and go get them. It's already yours...so OWN it.

THE CAGED FREE HEART

Letting Go of the Past that Incarcerates

2nd Edition

Dr. Trillion Small, LMFT

Order *The Caged Free Heart* on Amazon

The tug of war between your heart and mind can be one of the greatest battles you will ever have to fight. It is sometimes a fight that leaves us mentally and emotionally bound and metaphorically speaking, incarcerated. But that doesn't have to be how your story ends. If you are searching for mental and emotional freedom this book is for you. This book will help you to:

•Let go of those past pains that are keeping you bound

•Learn how to focus on the present instead of being anxious about tomorrow

•Find the mental and emotional freedom you desire

•Learn how to effectively "re-enter" into the world of relationships without fear and hidden barriers.

True clarity, peace, and freedom awaits you! This is your guide to finding your heart's wings!

INTERNAL NAVIGATOR

BASIC STEPS TO GET YOU FROM POINT A TO POINT B IN YOUR LIFE

2ND EDITION

TRILLION SMALL, PH.D.

Order *Internal Navigator* on Amazon

A revised edition. In 2013, Internal Navigator began as a guide to discovering and operating fully in your purpose. This second edition expands to include topics of emotional intelligence, psychological hardiness, and mental clutter extraction, to name a few. All in which are much needed on any journey that you embark upon. Just like a navigational system, you have to have a clear understanding of where you currently are and where you desire to go. Getting from Point A to Point B isn't the problem; it's what happens in between both points that can lead to stress, confusion, and fatigue. This book will serve as your personal guide by helping you know what to expect and how to prepare for your unique journey up ahead. Whether you are embarking on a personal, professional, or relationship journey, this book is for you. The scenario may be the same but the principles remain the same.

Continue the Discussion

Visit my website to book me to speak.

Sign up for my newsletter on my website.

Website: www.trillionsmall.com

Instagram: https://www.instagram.com/trillionsmall

Facebook: https://www.facebook.com/TrillionSmall

Twitter: https://twitter.com/trillionsmall

Youtube: https://www.youtube.com/trillionsmall

TEDxFrisco: www.TEDxFriscotx.com

Purchase the book from my website if you would like a personally autographed copy.